MW00626326

THE NEXT STEP

IN

HUMAN

EVOLUTION

THE NEXT STEP

IN

HUMAN

EVOLUTION

Scott Werner, MD

Tru Publishing
2939 S Mayflower Way,
Boise ID 83709

Copyright © 2015 by Scott Werner, M.D.

All rights reserved.

Published by Tru Publishing. No part of this book may be reproduced or transmitted in any form or by any means, electronic or mechanical, including photocopying, recording, or by any information storage and retrieval system, without written permission from the publisher. For more information, address Tru Publishing, 2939 S Mayflower Way, Boise ID 83709. Visit the Tru Publishing website at www.TruPublishing.com

Library of Congress Control Number: 2015936683

ISBN (paperback): 978-1-941420-06-5
1 2 3 4 5 6 19 18 17 16 15

1st edition, April 2015

Printed in the United States of America

Edited by Marilyn King, Ph.D. –
        www.BlueLotusEditing.com

DISCLAIMER

The author of this book does not dispense medical advice or prescribe the use of any technique as a form of treatment for physical, emotional, or medical problems without the advice of a physician, either directly or indirectly. The intent of the author is only to offer information of a general nature to help you in your quest for emotional and spiritual well-being. In the event that you use any of the information in this book for yourself, which is your constitutional right, the author and the publisher assume no responsibility for your actions.

DEDICATION

I would like to dedicate this book to my sweet wife Vicki and all ten of my children who have been patient with a busy husband and father, going off to other parts of the world doing sacred ceremonies, learning about plant medicine, chasing down fairies, elves and other mystical creatures, and now being the servant of Archangels and ascended Masters.

I would also like to thank Beverly Collins with her Ohana as she created the perfect space for St. Germaine to bring faith, hope and love in the writing of this book, MaDonna Mae for introducing the Sacred Flame decrees, Kevin and Stephanie Mullani for publishing and preparing the book, and Dr. Marilyn King for editing it.

Thank you all for being my loving family, friends, associates and fellow caretakers of this beautiful planet we all call home.

TABLE OF CONTENTS

INTRODUCTION

Connection to Fairfield, Iowa

Back in January 2011, my wife Vicki and I were making plans to travel to Europe to open a medical practice in San Tropez, or another nice town on the French Riviera. My daughter was in Geneva, Switzerland so we planned to travel with her, utilizing her knowledge of the French language. The exchange rate on the Euro was 1.6 to 1.0 dollar at the time, so we changed the amount of a $1.00 bill to $10,000.00 and placed it on my vision board to manifest extra money to help cover expenses for our trip. I didn't have to wait long for results.

I was in the middle of a dream where Maharishi Mahesh Yogi was asking me to go to Fairfield, Iowa to "detox my people" when a telephone call woke me up. It was a resident of Fairfield whom I had helped detox over the previous six months. She was calling to see if I would come to Fairfield and assist some of her friends to detox and lose weight. The group offered to cover my travel expenses and pay $100.00 each for a spiritual consultation. I didn't know how many people were interested, but I accepted, knowing the funds would help with our trip to Europe.

I ended up seeing 108 people, earning the desired amount of money and taking a wonderful trip to the French Riviera, but I didn't stay in Europe. Instead, I continued to go to Fairfield twice a year, to help "detox the people."

During my most recent visit to Fairfield, I lectured about our toxic environment covering topics such as herbicides, pesticides and radiation levels which are damaging our bodies and increasing infertility, auto-immune diseases, food allergies, immunity problems, organ failure and cancer rates.

The people of Fairfield had recently fought, protested and lost a battle over grain silo placement in their community. The farming corporations had built these silos in close proximity to Fairfield, and every time the grain harvest was put into these silos for storage until transportation, a heavy dust of chemical toxins (Glyphosate, Dicamba, and 2, 4-D), now being used to desiccate the plants to make harvesting easier, spread out for ten square miles, causing the population to become sick.

They asked after the lecture, "What do we do? You come and help us detox, only to have chemicals raining upon us." I couldn't give them a definitive answer, but I did say, "I think it will involve humans evolving so the toxins don't affect us." I planned a return trip to Fairfield the first part of October, 2014 to continue helping the people detox – and hopefully provide an actionable answer to their question.

I had to cancel my flight and delay my visit to Fairfield, however, because my sister-in-law, Angela Mandato, made arrangements for me to speak near Mt. Shasta at the Visionaries in Light Convergence on the same dates as my trip.

Angela was asked by Marilyn Harper to speak at the Visionaries in Light Convergence with Joeaux Robey, BJ King, Jamye Price and others. My wife's twin sister Syndi was also going to maintain a booth for Catherine Ann Clemett, another speaker, to help sell her books and other materials at the conference. In order to get me to take time off from my business, Health & Longevity, Inc., and because my goal is to speak at more conferences, Angela convinced Marilyn I should also speak at the conference because of several recent mystical events under my belt.

This was divinely inspired, as I had to receive the answer to their question prior to my return to Fairfield.

Food Allergy Epidemic Hits Home

The week prior to the speaking engagement at Mt. Shasta, my wife Vicki became ill due to food allergies and gluten contamination. She wanted to go to Mt. Shasta with us, but her body wasn't going to allow it this time.

Two years prior, in June 2012, Vicki had been hit with the perfect storm of health concerns. After getting an intestinal parasite in Peru, which lowered her immune response, and contracting a mutated gram-negative bacterial infection of the intestines (Escherichia Coli), which caused intermittent nausea, vomiting, and loose stools for three months, her nervous system was extra susceptible to another attack.

Then, in November 2012, a heavy dose of chemtrails rained down upon our hometown of St. George, Utah. Chemtrails are the long lasting trails in the sky left from aircraft, comprised of chemical or biological agents, and deliberately delivered for testing their effects on the unsuspecting population below. This particular mixture contained a mutated adenovirus (glandular virus), inside atypical bacteria called mycoplasma pneumonia. This virus invaded Vicki's lungs and blood stream, then penetrated her sympathetic nervous system causing hyper-stimulation of the autonomic fight or flight response. The parasympathetic nervous system, or vagus nerve response of digest, rest, rebuild and repair, would never trigger in this hyper-stimulatory state, causing her body to eat her own muscles and other tissues in order to stay alive.

Add to this a severe gluten intolerance that developed into leaky gut syndrome. This condition occurs when macromolecules of undigested foods "leak" through holes in the small intestine, getting into the bloodstream. The immune system then attacks these undigested food particles, causing allergic reactions to what would normally be wonderful, organic food.

Bone broth, a convalescing soup broth of cooked meat, organs and bones, became Vicki's only friend to mend and repair the intestinal villi. She would drink this broth every time she would become sick to stop the body from eating itself and to stay alive. We also found that avoiding any foods that caused a reaction (determined by blood analysis at ALCAT labs), only eating the seven foods she wasn't allergic to (the short green list), and taking Slippery Elm and Skull Cap herbs were all very helpful in calming down her system.

Vicki's recovery regimen required constant attention and she could not travel or eat out at restaurants. So, instead of traveling to Mt. Shasta, the severity of her reaction caused her to stay home with our two youngest children to mend. I still had a commitment to speak though, so Angela, Syndi and I started out from St. George, Utah on a trip that would change our lives.

Scott Werner, MD

CHAPTER 1

Meeting St. Germaine

We stopped at midnight in Reno, Nevada on our way to Mt. Shasta. The "girls" liked to stop and see the scenic views, which had turned a ten-hour drive into fourteen. Too tired to go on, and with six hours more of driving ahead, I searched the internet for a place to stay. Circus Circus was the least expensive, so I clicked purchase on my phone. Angela just wanted to lie down for two hours and get back on the road, while I was ready for a longer nap. She had signed up to take the $150.00, 9:00 AM tour of Mt. Shasta with the main group at the pre-conference event. Syndi and I were too cheap, so we made other plans. Despite my objection, alarm blaring at 2:00 AM, I dragged my tired body out of bed to continue our journey.

For three years I had desired to experience Mt. Shasta, after reading the St. Germaine "I Am" series of books. More recently, I also had read a book about the 3rd & 5th dimensional beings of Telos, a mystical advanced society of peaceful, tall (14-16 feet) blonde humanoids living underneath the mountain, which had piqued my interest in finding the entrance and traveling inside the mountain as well.

Three weeks prior to visiting Mt. Shasta, I had a dream, showing me the entrance to a cave, which would lead down into the mountain, down to another civilization. It was near the headwaters of the Sacramento River. In the dream, there were two large boulders with a flattened area in between, filled with old bark, and roots hanging down the front of the flattened area. I was to sit on the bark between the two rocks and meditate, with the intent to receive permission for entrance. If entrance was permitted, the boulder to the right, as if on a hinge, would lift up, and I would enter the cavern, following it down to Telos.

We arrived at 6:30 AM, thanks to the speedy driving of Syndi, who handled the truck like a professional racecar driver, getting us to the Mt. Shasta City Park earlier than expected. Angela had fallen into a deep sleep in the back seat. I jumped out to find the headwaters of the Sacramento River, located in the city park. A hundred feet to the east, at a sign stating I was at the Headwaters of the Sacramento River, I filled my water bottle with the cold clear water coming directly from the base of the mountain. A young woman was doing her yoga on the concrete pad next to the water's edge. I nodded, "Good Morning," then started my search for the rocks in my dream.

To my chagrin, after searching for an hour and a half, the rocks and entrance in my dream were nowhere to be found. I headed back to the Mt. Shasta City Park, discouraged.

Next to the spring waters, an older man in a grey hoody jacket with a long grey beard was filling his water containers. I felt a tingle and warmth in my Solar Plexus, which told me there was something special about this man, even though he looked to be a homeless person.

I approached him and out of my mouth came the question, "Do you know where the entrance to Telos is?" A big toothy smile appeared, brightening his bearded face. "Why yes," he grinned, "but it's not here." "There is another headwaters spring up near the tree line summit by Upper Panther Meadows," he explained, still grinning ear to ear. "You will find what you seek 200 yards to the east of the spring."

The next question springing forth from my soul to my mouth was, "Have you met the Telos, or any other aliens?" Again he grinned, stating, "Why, yes! Over 21 different species from all over the galaxy," which sent my mind reeling. "How could this be?" I thought. I then proceeded to ask him about what types, how many, what were they doing here? I also asked about "Big Foot" who had first been documented as being seen at Mt Shasta. The only question I missed, in an hour while I conversed with this spindly older gentleman, was "What is your name?"

Being deep in conversation, I hadn't noticed a crowd was gathering around us. The bearded gentleman smiled, bidding me "Good luck in your searching," then disappeared in the crowd.

I called Vicki on my cell phone to tell her of the bearded man and the amazing conversation. She, being sensitive to energy, stated, "I feel like you just spoke with St. Germaine." She asked, "Is he still around?" I answered, "He disappeared into the crowd.

CHAPTER 2

Mt. Shasta

Marilyn Harper climbed up on the rocks at the headwaters for the Sacramento River and announced, "We welcome you to Mt. Shasta, a mystical mountain, and the perfect location for the Visionaries in Light Convergence."

My mind was still centered on finding the entrance to Telos. I told Syndi my plan to head up the mountain and find Upper Panther Meadows. She was in complete agreement, so we jumped into my red Silverado pickup truck.

In my rush to get going, I hadn't realized how hungry I was. I also didn't know where I was headed. Syndi and I drove back into town, looking for somewhere to eat and get some coffee, as I was feeling the effects from 2 hours sleep. We found a quaint little coffee and donut house, which just happened to make eggs, toast and hash browns with a delicious salsa for breakfast.

I asked a local man, "Which road will take us to Upper Panther Meadows?" He answered, "Just get on A-10, Everitt Memorial Highway, and go all the way up into the National Forest, past Lower Panther Meadows about thirteen miles." "Wow," I thought. "I'm being guided all the way. What if I get into the mountain, and I don't find my way out?" I thought as I went into fear. Fear always holds us back from what we should be doing, I thought, remembering the lessons I had learned writing my first book.

While Syndi finished up her breakfast and headed into the bathroom, I was making up my mind about Telos. Little did I know, that decision had already been made for me.

CHAPTER 3

The Telos

Driving up into the National Forest was a pleasure. Pine trees smelled fresh and looked beautiful. I've always enjoyed nature. Growing up, instead of going to church, my parents loved to gather up the kids and head to the mountain, to hunt, fish, gather wood, or just go on a hike.

The road twisted and turned as we climbed Mt. Shasta, and the air became cooler and more crisp. At last, I spotted a National Forest sign with the words Lower Panther Meadows, which meant we were almost there. The timberline was close, the trees became sparser, and the paved road ended. We pulled the truck off to the right side in a parking area. The mountain loomed in the background, going up more than 4,000 feet higher. Igneous rocks, and plenty of them, were piled all over.

Staying below the trees, we walked to the south, staying on the upper trail the happy bearded man had told me about. Sure enough, there it was: the higher spring, and headwaters to the Sacramento River, a rounded dry spring at this time of the year, with just grass vegetation surrounding it and igneous rock within it.

My mission was to find the two rocks I had seen in my dream. Walking to the east, I paced off about 150 yards, and there it was, just as I had envisioned: a place with two large boulders, with trees on both sides, bark filling the empty space between them, and roots hanging down below the bark and the boulders.

I marveled at how my dream had been so accurate. The happy bearded man at the lower springs had told me to sit down on the bark and meditate, asking for admission. There was a perfect spot in the middle of the rocks, so I sat in prayer pose, and began meditating. Syndi, in her nervous way, continued to hike around on the mountain.

As I calmed my mind, just enjoying the serenity of the mountain, colors and lights started to dance around me. The elementals energy presented itself, bringing joy and bliss as I continued to go deeper into super-consciousness. Then, I heard a voice speak as clearly as if they were standing close to me, "Scott, we know why you have come on this journey, and we appreciate your thoughts and desires of visiting our home. The humans in charge are not yet ready for our civilization to come out, and we do not desire for them to find us until they evolve, becoming peaceful, not filled with hatred and fear. If your government found us now in their primitive state, they would study us with their so-called scientists, take our technology, interrogate us, then kill us as they have so many they call aliens. Today is not the day for you to enter the mountain, there are too many witnesses who could see you enter, and they would come with their machinery, digging out the entrance, and invade our home. We will do an energy healing on your body as you sit and meditate."

Syndi reappeared and asked, "Can I sit and meditate with you?" She then sat down behind me, with her back against mine. As we meditated together, the violet flame appeared and started from the base or root chakra, and moved itself up through the crystalline chamber through all the chakras in my body. I heard St. Germaine's voice say, "Thank you for coming to my favorite mountain." I said, "Thank you for inviting me."

I felt the lower back tingle with light energy, which took away some minor discomfort of the long drive. Syndi had been experiencing some spasms in her back and kidneys, which were relieved with the same energy. For a few seconds in the violet flame, I could see three beings, St. Germaine, St. Michael, and Archangel Gabriel. Syndi and I were both grateful, and hungry for lunch. What had seemed like 15-20 minutes to me had actually been three hours.

We started hiking back to the road, when a lady approached us and we had the following conversation: Woman: "I was meditating by the spring head of the Sacramento River, when I heard St. Germaine state, 'Go visit with the couple at the entrance to Telos. Tell them of your experiences to increase their hope and faith.'"

I started to tell her of the experience we just went through. After telling her, she laughed and said, "I've been coming here for over 25 years, for a month each fall, to meditate, ask questions and heal with the energy you just spoke about. I currently live in Hawaii the rest of the year."

She then started explaining how St. Germaine is helping the whole planet, plants, animals, and all smaller organisms, including all the humans, to evolve, explaining the importance of connecting to our higher self through meditation, quieting the mind, and pulling ourselves out of the matrix of energy controlling our lives.

She further explained how the humans who think they are in control keep us in the matrix, through our electronic devices, the media, government agencies, and mostly through fear. Since September 11, 2001, the combined vibration of humanity has dropped precipitously and though many of us are waking up, the light workers and beings of light have stepped up the work of raising the vibration of the earth and humans back up, so we collectively can evolve, which is better than stagnation, fear, pain and death.

As souls, she said, when we are not progressing and evolving, we are suffering with diseases, pain and mental disorders, especially anxiety, depression, psychosis, shame, blame, and guilt. These low vibrating emotions lead to a lack of self-love, leading to lowered immunity to parasites, fungi, atypical bacterial infections, and chronic viruses, which can enter our bodies without restraint. We seek help from the Medical System, who treat the body with chemotherapy, surgery, removing diseased organs, and prescribing pharmaceutical drugs that mask the symptoms, not treating the mental, physical and emotional core causes of diseases. These drugs, in combination with the chemicals and toxins being put into our food, water and air, further deteriorate our physical defenses and immune systems, leading to cancer and chronic inflammatory illnesses which have never existed before on the planet. This further discourages us, putting us into despair, making us more susceptible to mind control, turning us into drones, doing the will of those who are causing the problems in the first place.

St. Germaine has come up with a beautiful positive plan, she told us, using all the beings of light, the Healing Masters, the Star Children, Cosmic sacred flames and beings, the Archangels, elemental beings, Arcturians, Andromedans, Orion council of light, Pleiadians, and other species from all the other worlds in the universe who have evolved to the next level, to help us to evolve and continue our growth and destiny. It will involve cleansing and removing parasites, re-educating, un-brainwashing, helping the masses understand who they are and why they are really here on earth, and giving them peace, hope and faith. But most Divine, it will involve teaching the people love consciousness.

As she finished this information and more, I marveled how many people are waking up. Many of the things she said I have believed for a long time, but to have it all spelled out so beautifully and concisely helped me to know I was on my path. Now, it was lunchtime.

CHAPTER 4

The Arkansas House

Syndi and I were cold. We wanted some hot food and a place to sit in the sun. Driving back down the mountain into Mt. Shasta City, we found Lalo's Mexican restaurant. We sat down outside, in the sun, feeling the bliss of the town. The food we ordered was wolfed down, and filled our tummies and our souls. We both fell into a magical sleep for about thirty minutes with our heads resting back against the building. We awoke refreshed and satisfied. Once we were up, we paid the bill and we were leaving when the group who had taken the formal tour returned.

We asked them, one by one, "How was your tour?" Most of them responded, "Not as I had expected." Syndi's and my experience had been amazing.

Angela, Catherine and her fiancé, David, arrived, and their experience had been like the others, not anything special; everyone was tired, and they were all ready to take a nap.

We had a room at a house in town that had eight rooms with two beds in each room. There were twelve people from Arkansas, so we called the home "Arkansas House." There were people from all over the country staying at the house, as well as one person from Belgium.

He was always so happy, and everyone enjoyed his being there.

We were all like-minded, light-hearted and jovial. All of us became great friends immediately, sharing our experiences and stories. Syndi and I found our rooms and quietly rested from the day that had started so early. Dreams of the Telos still filled my head; a light dream of entering the mountain started again, and soon I found myself surrounded with the beautiful tall beings of light.

I awoke about 8:00 PM to the sound of light drumming. Someone was tuning their drums. As I headed down the stairs, I could see that Syndi and Angela were still sleeping soundly in their room. Three Trees, obviously not his given name (Jeff Strong), was setting up his orchestra of instruments, including a didgeridoo. Someone had asked him to do a clearing concert for the house and all the people in it, and his playing was incredible. It was so loud, I thought for sure Angela and Syndi would have awakened to join us. He played for about two hours. When he played the didgeridoo, he started at the feet of each person and ended up at the heart chakra. I was at the end of the line, and he finally arrived at my feet, working up my body. By the time he played the instrument at my heart, a meditative state came upon me, and I couldn't sit, so I headed up to my bed, fell into a deep sleep, with the beautiful tall beings of light waving their hands over my body again.

CHAPTER 5

A Warning

I was one of the first to wake up on October 10th. It was still dark, around 5:00 AM, and the house was still sleeping. I quietly closed the front door, stepping out into the early morning darkness. Should I head back up Mt. Shasta to see if the Telos would let me in? Then a woman stepped out and asked, "Would you care to take a walk?" I answered, "Sure." "I guess there are more days left to go up Mt. Shasta," I thought, not speaking.

"So you want to meet the Telos?" she questioned. "Why yes," I answered. She seemed to know my thoughts. "You probably wouldn't be able to come back," she stated. "What do you mean?" I questioned back. "Many have gone into the mountain, but few have returned," she answered. "I wanted to go into the mountain, but was told by my guides I wouldn't return on this dimension. I could only appear to warn others, so they, didn't make the same decision unknowingly." I looked ahead of us for a moment, contemplating what she had just said. I turned my head back to the left, to ask her how she knew what I was thinking, and she was gone.

I felt a little freaked out. What had just happened? Did she really come out of the house or did I just imagine talking with someone just now? My reality was shaken, but the early morning fresh air was real, it was chilly and yes, I needed my jacket. My heart was racing so I said to myself, "Peace, be still," three times to calm my heart and body. I had learned this technique from my guides to calm my nervous system and heart.

Two thousand years ago, when the disciples were traveling on the Sea of Galilee, "A furious squall came up, and the waves broke over the boat, so that it was nearly swamped." Mark 3:37. Others were on even smaller boats, following Jesus, and those little boats were also taking on water, so the disciples, fearing for all their lives, awoke Jesus, who was lying asleep on a pillow, saying "Master, thou carest not that we perish?" And Jesus arose and rebuked the wind and said unto the sea, "Peace, be still."

Whenever our nerves or our bodies are in a nervous "storm," "Peace, be still," stated three times, will calm us instantly.

Being several blocks from the house, I continued to walk, knowing my time to go into the mountain wouldn't be for a long time.

CHAPTER 6

The Archangel Cards

I arrived back at the house about 6:30 AM, and people were in the kitchen making breakfast and getting ready for the day. I was invited to have a bowl of oatmeal, which I readily accepted. A lady who wasn't from Arkansas House had some colorful laminated cards she was showing to people. I asked, "What are these used for?" She answered, "They have been channeled to a lady out of Colorado. They have been infused with the Sacred Flame energies of the beings of light, the Archangels, Ascended Masters and others. Hold them to see which one you are attracted to."

It was a fairly thick stack of 130 cards, 8 ½ x 11 inches in size. As I went through the cards, I became focused on the card bearing the image of Archangel Zaphkiel, "Angel of Compassion and Ecstasy, keeper of the Orange Flame of the Sacral Plexus chakra."

Three years previous to this encounter, while I had been ill with pancreatitis or worse, a psychic lady had told me, "They have stolen your orange flame!" "Who are they?" I thought. "Why did they pick me? What does that even mean?" It had taken years to figure out what she had meant, and here I was faced with Archangel Zaphkiel, keeper of the Orange Flame of the Sacral Plexus chakra.

"Go ahead," she stated, handing me the stack of cards with Archangel Zaphkiel on the top. "Stand with your bare feet on the cards." Doing what I was told, I took my socks off, and proceeded to place my bare feet on the cards.

Within a millisecond, my feet started to burn, then felt like they were on fire. I jumped off the cards. "What was that?" I almost screamed with the intensity. "Seems like that is definitely the card you need," she laughed deeply. "Step back on. I'll ask them to go easier on you," she stated, still laughing.

It took me a minute to gather the courage to step back onto the cards. My feet and calves had tenderness and burning from a neuropathy that had been developing over the past three years. Pancreatic proteases and other enzymes produced in the pancreas had backed up due to a stone in the "Ampulla of Vater," and pancreatitis ensued, digesting many of the cells in my pancreas including the "islets of Langerhans" or beta cells, which lowered my insulin production. I had never gone to the medical establishment, because I didn't want to be labeled with a diagnosis of pancreatitis or worse.

At the time, I knew intuitively exactly what had happened. I had been in horrible central abdominal pain, waking up early December 15th of 2011, feeling like a knife was being twisted and turned in my pancreas. It woke me up, and I had asked my guides, "What is going on?" They spoke to my mind saying, "Pancreatitis."

"What do I do?" I asked. "You have two choices, go the hospital where you eventually will have a 'Whipple' procedure, end up with a post-surgical infection and die in three months. The other choice is to go to the 'Big Island' of Hawaii, and eat organic pineapple, papaya, and passion fruit. Visit with Pe'le up in the caldera of the volcano, and ask her to heal your pancreas and pop out the stone."

Obviously, I liked the second option best, to take the red pill, getting outside of the matrix.

Barbara, my wife's sister, came over to the house for coffee that morning, telling Vicki that six of them were going to Hawaii and flying into Kona from Los Angeles the next morning. Hearing this, I asked, "Can we go? Do you have any more tickets?" She stated, "No. My friend only has six for me." I asked, "Can you get any more?" "I can call and ask," she replied.

I just knew my angels were working things out. She got off the phone with her friend and laughed, "His boss just gave him two 1st class upgrades this morning and he can't use them, so he'd be happy to give them to me/you." We filled the red truck with our luggage and drove down to LAX that day. We checked into the Hilton at LAX to await our flight.

The next morning, we flew to Kona, on the big Island of Hawaii, where we found abundant fresh pineapple and passion fruit and picked papaya right off the trees. We traveled up to the Volcano National Park, hiked down into the caldera of the Kīlauea Iki Crater, did toning (God sounds) and prayers in the crater which vibrated the stone free from the ampulla of Vater, allowing the pancreatic juices to flow out, instead of being backed up into my pancreas and digesting the same organ.

Now, back in Mt. Shasta, I carefully stepped back onto the Archangel cards, with the Archangel Zaphkiel card on top. The intensity of the next five minutes carried hot energy at first, then warm healing energy from the bottom of my feet to my pelvis and more. I quit complaining, and instead started rejoicing in the wondrous changes I was experiencing. I could feel the nerves repairing, the tissues healing, the blood flowing and the lymph moving, but most of all, the orange flame rekindling in my Sacral Plexus. I thought, "I better get me a set of these cards."

CHAPTER 7

Visionaries in Light Convergence
October, 2014

Weed, California, located in Siskiyou County, is an interesting little town with a population of fewer than 3,000. It is named after a local pioneer and lumber mill builder, Abner Weed, not Marijuana as many think. Higher education is at the College of the Siskiyou, and this is where the Visionaries in Light Convergence was located.

We walked in about 8:30 AM and immediately my attention was drawn to a woman with auburn hair, setting up her booth on the right. I wandered over to start up a conversation and immediately she started to speak Elfin, an ancient light language, which amazingly enough to me, I understood. Translating the language she said, "Welcome to the Inter-Galactic Federation, we are so glad you decided to come, old friend. It's been a long time. As king of the elves, let me be the first to greet you, and thank you for your desires to bring knowledge, light and love to the humans on this planet." She then started crying tears of joy, saying, "I know you have suffered, but the suffering is over, and it is time to rejoice and heal our worlds, re-establishing our friendship and alliance."

Jamye Price then came back into her body, still with tears in her eyes, asking, "Who are you?" "My name is

Scott Werner, but I guess I'm not really sure who I am after that introduction," I answered.

Jamye and I then went on talking about the elfin language she had just spoken, a language possibly channeled by John Ronald Reuel Tolkien (1892-1973) who was a major scholar of the English language, specializing in Old and Middle English. Professor of Anglo-Saxon (Old English) at the University of Oxford, he also wrote a number of stories, including most famously *The Hobbit* (1937) and *The Lord of the Rings* (1954-1955), which are set in a pre-historic era in an invented version of our world, which he called by the Middle English name of Middle-earth. He, being a linguist, possibly created "Elfin," a language that actually may have been taught to him by his mother, who was interested in linguistics, and who died in his younger years.

Jamye and I became friends immediately. I felt an instant camaraderie, like there was some past life connection. Throughout the conference, I would sit and talk with her, learning about what she does to heal people. She brings in this "Language of Light," the most spoken universal language, which can shift the energy within the subtle astral and etheric bodies and the emotional and spiritual energies, aligning them with our soul purpose.

We went on discussing how love is the solution for everything, and we can use this powerful energy to create our reality. It will leave behind and un-create wars, hatred, envy, lust, greed, fear, jealousy and all other negative emotions. Love creates faith, abundance, prosperity, cooperation, trust, healing and perfection. Through love, we are in control of our own evolution first, and then, as we evolve, our world will follow. "The light of love is burning all the darkness away," Jayme said.

"The key to higher existence is to set your intent on higher love frequencies, which create higher frequencies in our bodies, which evolve us faster," stated Jayme. We also discussed how Spiritual energy is also powerful to heal character defects, which plague many of us. As we transform with love and the higher frequencies, we no longer crave cigarettes, alcohol, drugs, pornography, lustful thoughts and depraved sex. We love others, and ourselves so crime, burglaries, abuse, and injuring or murdering others never becomes a thought or reality.

Imagine a world where everyone is manifesting love and higher frequencies, a flowering of consciousness, if you will. The higher energy of creation is producing free energy through innovations and machines tapping into "zero point" devices, magnetic generators, motion pulsed generators, motionless pulsed generators, gravitational pulsed systems, battery charging pulsed systems, energy-tapping pulsed systems, electrostatic generators, and many others, producing clean, efficient energy to run our homes, businesses, farms, gathering areas, etc. This would free us from the greenhouse gases of petroleum, natural gas and coal, let alone toxic nuclear energy.

Laughter instead of violence would fill the entertainment industry. Laughter has been shown to oxygenate the blood, open up the lymphatics, improve attitude and emotions, building good energy in the body, and it also feeds the quantum field with optimism.

We finished our discussion, feeling refreshed and happy to have met each other.

The next three days filled us with love and optimism.

CHAPTER 8

Leaving Mt. Shasta

It was a crispy cool bright morning. Mt. Shasta majestically loomed in the east, with the sun breaking over the southern ridge. Many who had attended the Visionaries in Light Convergence sipped their coffee and tea, hovering over the kitchen oven, muffins baking inside, as the house had not warmed up yet.

We had jointly called the home the Arkansas House, because the females, who were the majority in the house, were from Arkansas. As a group, we had occupied this quaint two-story house, with eight small rooms, with double the beds, for the past four days. We discussed and pondered about all the amazing speakers who had delivered messages of peace and hope for the people of planet earth at the conference. I especially felt the presence of spiritual Masters as I took another swallow of the delightful dark brew.

My life as a spiritual medical intuitive led to a fascination with all sacred locations on the planet. As a trained Medical Doctor, I had my scientifically skeptical side, always looking for self-actualization and Newtonian proof (through the five physical senses) of the validity of these mystical vortices.

My sister-in-law, Angela Mandato, a Peruvian trained Shaman by calling, a massage therapist by trade, had been asked to speak by Marilyn Harper, a channel of Adironnda, a Master teacher from another time and place. Angela, by speaking so highly of me, had gotten a 22-minute slot for me to tell some of my story, which is why I had been at the conference.

The past four days had been filled with wonder, courage, and peace. To my amazement, I had felt another shift in my own consciousness, bringing more faith, peace and love, and a higher desire to be of service. My whole life I had felt I was serving, being a healer and physician, but now I could feel something else coming, another level of service, but I was unsure what it would be.

Angela and Syndi had both wanted to experience Stewart Mineral Springs, near Weed, California. We said our goodbyes to all our newfound friends, loaded up the red pickup, and headed north on I-5, to find Stewart Mineral Springs.

Traveling west on Stewart Springs Road for four miles, we found the springs, with many small buildings and ponds nearby. It was 9:00 AM in the morning, so the springs were closed and didn't open for 2 more hours. I was anxious to be driving home, but I also wanted to go to The *McCloud River*, and to the falls, which is one of California's aquatic jewels. Located near the top of California, with headsprings coming from Mt. Shasta, they are the starting places for many rivers, north of the

Sierra Nevada and at the southern end of the Cascade Range of volcanic mountains.

Several of the conference attendees had gone to the McCloud River, and had photographed and seen with their eyes and cameras, fairies, which I was highly interested in seeing myself. It was south of Mt. Shasta, and on our way home. I convinced Angela and Syndi to get on the road, and not to wait for two additional hours for the springs to open, just so we could soak for another two hours. Syndi also had called a friend, who would be waiting in Reno for a dinner date. So she was more than willing to get going.

We first reached McCloud, stopped and got gas and some coffee. We then headed southeast on California state road 89. We stopped at the lower falls first, taking as many pictures as we could, hoping to catch orbs and fairies. We then proceeded to the middle falls and then on to the upper falls. At the upper falls, we were walking to the river outlook, when all of a sudden Angela took a nasty fall, spraining her ankle. It hurt so intensely, she thought it was broken. I examined it, felt the energy, and told her, "It's just a bad sprain." Her knee and lower leg were bleeding, making it look bad. She couldn't stand up on it, so I had her just relax on the ground, removed the traumatic energy from the ankle, and started to send healing energy to reduce the pain and swelling to her knee, lower leg, and ankle.

Angela remarked, "It's just like something grabbed my ankle, causing me to fall." With that statement, I looked into the energy, and found she was right; something or someone had energetically pulled at her ankle, resulting in her rolling on the ankle and falling. I said, "Put protection around your body, with the Archangels, and put stealth energy around your body, so only beings of higher frequency can see and assist you." I also did the same for myself. The energy surrounding us both improved from fear to peace.

I left Angela in the care of the angels and healing Masters, sitting on a rock to recover for a few moments.

Syndi had disappeared, hiking down a dirt path, off the main path. Keeping Angela in sight, still sending comfort and healing energy, I looked down at the beautiful clear river, seeing nature at its best. The blue sky and air were pristine, and the sounds from the waterfalls cascading over the rocks, along with the lush green and browns of the plants and earth, all deepened the call to protect nature. The beauty was breathtaking. I had previously helped people heal, especially out in nature.

I walked back to Angela, telling her of the beauty of the falls and the river, helped her to get back on her feet, and suggested, "Let's just take a few minutes and meditate over by the falls." She became excited to do this, as meditation accelerates healing. "We should ask the plants, the creatures, the rocks, and earth to assist you with their energy, not enough to affect them, but just a small amount from all that we see, to heal your leg and ankle." We both sat down on a bench over by the falls, letting our minds connect with nature's beauty. Instantly, pain was forgotten, and bliss entered in.

Syndi reappeared and said, "I want you to follow me down this trail." Angela just desired to sit and heal, so I said to Syndi, "I'll come with you." As we proceeded down a dirt trail along the ridge above the river, leading further down the river to the lower falls, the incline became slanted, making even my footing unsteady. I looked back and Angela had followed, but I was concerned about her leg and ankle, so I went back to assist her. Angela was interested in what Syndi had seen, but I didn't want Angela to roll her ankle again. I started taking as many pictures as I could, fully expecting to get some photos of the fairies in this wondrous place in nature, as I guided Angela back to the truck. Angela and I never did see what Syndi had seen.

CHAPTER 9

St. Germaine Materializes

The rest of the trip to Reno was unremarkable. Syndi was driving, so we arrived quickly and easily. Angela lay down in the back seat, with her leg and ankle elevated. We arrived around 5:00 PM. Syndi had made a dinner date with a friend of all of ours, Mike Taggett, who had lived in LaVerkin Utah, where Syndi's whole family lived. He had moved to Reno several years earlier, for another adventure in business. He is the entrepreneur who started Chums, which is a cloth material that retains a strong hold onto your eyewear.

I searched for a hotel for the night and was able to get a great room for us at the Silver Legacy Resort & Casino, for $36.00 on October 13, 2014. Why am I giving such detailed information? Because what happened that night was amazing – and occurred right in a room at the hotel and casino.

I was a little hyper and wasn't ready for bed, so I stayed up and wandered around the casino, watching people and looking for a possible machine that was ready for a jackpot. I kept testing with my intuition, but all the machines were not giving, but receiving that night, so after 20 minutes I went back up to the room.

Having had such an amazing spiritual experience the past five days left me with so much gratitude, I started to pray and meditate when I arrived in the room. I quickly fell asleep.

I awoke, feeling a presence in the room. I first looked over at the clock, which said 2:22 AM. Looking toward my feet, at the end of the bed, I could feel warm energy, and a purple, violet essence forming. Then, very gently, an image of a man appeared, walking toward me in the energy, with love exuding toward me. As he walked through this portal, he ended up at the end of my bed.

"I am St. Germaine, and I have come to you, Scott Werner, as you are an open vessel, with answers to the questions you and others have had in your thoughts and your minds over the past six months. The meditating population on the planet is fully aware of the dangers in the pesticides, herbicides and radiation, being used on our foods. The chemical pollution in our atmosphere, from the corporate control of energy and chemical production, is at an all-time high, and getting worse. The releasing of chemical and biological agents, including mind control chemicals and toxins, immune system invaders, and biological warfare experimentation, right here in the United States, is being dropped by the tons through the chemtrails visible every week now. This is being done, with the end result of enslavement and mind control of the people of the freest country on planet earth. These agents are also causing sickness, cancer, DNA and RNA breakage and damage, disabilities, new 'auto-immune diseases' and an epidemic of what you call 'Alzheimer's disease' in adults and Asperger's spectrum and attention deficit disorder in our children and young adults, but are actually mind enslavement and control. These chemicals are being brought into our systems through the lungs with mutated atypical bacteria, such as mycobacteria, chlamydia, mycoplasma and others, with nano-bot technologies, with a genetically modified protease or enzyme which dissolves the membranes protecting our lungs and blood, allowing entrance of these diabolical creations of the corporate and military labs. From there, these organisms travel through the lymph and the blood, infecting cells throughout the body, and are also designed to weaken the immune system and natural defenses.

"The food is also being treated with these chemicals, toxins, viruses implanted to genetically change the food and alter our digestive systems, changing the normal bacterial flora, which is the first defense of our gut, causing all sorts of digestive issues, including leaky gut, food allergies, auto-immune diseases and nutrient breakdown and absorption problems. This in turn breaks down the villi in the absorptive areas of the gut, creating an environment of undigested foods allowing fungus to overwhelm the defenses, entering into the blood and body organs further weakening the immune system.

"But, you know all of this, Scott Werner, due to your open mind and studies, for which I am truly grateful," stated St. Germaine. "Your question has been troubling you for years: 'What can we do?' You go out and detox people, just to have them be exposed again and again, with newer evil inventions and created toxins every day, not to mention the highest levels of radiation and radioactive isotopes in our environment, causing DNA and RNA breakage daily.

"I come to you with an answer! Just as you said on your last visit and lecture in Fairfield, Iowa, in April 2014," he said, quoting my words in Fairfield, "'I believe we will have to evolve so these toxins, petrochemicals, radiation and germ warfare will not affect us.'

"You had the answer, but not the method," said St. Germaine. Continuing, he stated, "Evolution is the answer and is inevitable for survival on this beautiful planet. I will tell you how this is to be done."

St. Germaine continued, "Humans, in the beginning, were created in the image of God or source energy. Yes, there was a beginning of human beings. These first humans were perfect in every way, a reflection of the perfection and love of source, the God energy. Animal and plant life was also in a state of perfection and love in this spiritual realm. The first humans were in a state of bliss, compassion and perfect love, traveling the universe, through mind and telepathy for eons, until, feeling the need to expand themselves, outside of source (ego, a lower vibration and separation from source), created this and other universes. In the process, this dualistic three-dimensional universe was created and is full of opposites, as you well know.

"Just as the 'Gods,' as they called themselves, played with the universe creating and manifesting anything and everything that came into their consciousness, as they sank lower in their vibratory states, creations and dimensions vibrating at lower levels appeared. Their state of bliss and love disappeared, and the connection to the higher vibrating universes dissolved. That connection is in the DNA. The original humans had perfected DNA, which, in the form of the double helix with telomeres connected to the DNA, allowed them to connect to the multiverse and source energy, like little antennae, sending and receiving energy from source, making it simple to manifest and create. These 'God' people could communicate with other worlds, nations and each other by telepathy. (Telomeres at the ends of the DNA in their perfect state would never break, allowing for longer lives.)

"For our purposes, in this third dimension," St Germaine continued, "perfected humans first coming to this world from other places had 24 strands of DNA, which were in twelve double helixes, and braided into rope DNA. Genetic engineering, energy production, and other paths of technology had brought great wonders to the people of Planet Marduk, one of the places these humans came from, but they also presented problems. Simple mistakes by genetic engineers could produce bizarre mutations, and mistakes by energy researchers could cause powerful explosions. After a certain point, scientific technology on Marduk took on a life of its own, and there seemed to be no stopping it, even if the people had wanted to. The rewards of scientific achievement were absolutely wonderful, dwarfing the occasional accidents and potential dangers, or so the people thought.

"There are some who believe all our ancestors came from Marduk, which, previous to its destruction, was a heavily populated large planet (which many referred to as 'Eden' because of the lush and beautiful vegetation), orbiting between Mars and Jupiter; its destruction created the asteroid belt." St Germaine added, "Many beings from many planets and systems are ancestors to earth humans."

St Germaine continued, "When these Marduk humans were trapped on earth, due to the destruction of their own planet, they intermingled with their creations and primitive humanoids on earth; causing damage to the 12 double helix, 24 strand DNA was inevitable, because the gametes, or sperm and ovum, were unwound from the protection of the rope DNA, making it vulnerable to breakage and loss, especially when combined with other species with unperfected DNA of fewer strands. The 12 stranded sperm and egg could not continue and two stranded DNA humans was the result.

"These humans brought with them the technologies of Marduk, creating the societies of Lemuria and Atlantis with the technologies of genetic transfer, free-power, and replicator technologies, which made the societies powerful, but without restraint and conscious decision in the creations. For a thousand years, they lived in peace, until devices using radioactive isotopes and substances were created, which has effects on the entire multiverse and other dimensions, and further damaged the devolving human species with lower vibrations. War, greed, envy and power were constantly on the minds in this lower frequency. Humans were divided on who would benefit from this technology, causing further separation and strife. A world war broke out, using atomic power and artificial intelligence, which un-created these amazing civilizations, and also affected the civilizations on Venus and Mars."

CHAPTER 10

Artificial Intelligence

St. Germaine continued, "There is a project called 'Initiative 2045' that the scientific community of earth is currently spending billions of dollars on, which is going to create cyborgs or what they call avatar bodies in which they will put artificial intelligence technologies and human personalities, creating immortal beings which are actually only going to be used by the 'Cabal,' a small group of people who work together secretly controlling the planet. The billions of dollars could be used for alleviating the suffering and hunger of billions of people on the planet, cleaning up the environment, and moving forward with free energy, but the dark methods of the world's hidden government would rather use our greatest scientists and resources to create these 'immortal avatars' to place their personality and purported consciousness in, so they can continue to live forever. Their plan is actually to become the immortal masters of the planet, and enslave the rest of the population.

"This is a technology which has long implications, but needs to be addressed," St. Germaine continued. "The personalities of the 'hidden government' controllers are already filled with personality defects and anti-social and grandiose psychoses. They would add this to an immortal artificial intelligence, which is self-repairing, thinking it is a 'God' to and for humanity, but also being susceptible to the Demonic energies of getting pleasure from the torture and suffering they are already allowing on the planet."

St. Germaine then referred me to the website of the 2045 Initiative, http://2045.com/ideology/.

The website states the organization was, "Founded by Russian entrepreneur Dmitry Itskov in February 2011 with the participation of leading Russian specialists in the field of neural interfaces, robotics, artificial organs and systems." ("The founder of these ideas, Dmitry Itskov, is a Cabal enthusiast," stated St. Germaine.)

The main goals ("which are deceiving," said St. Germaine) of this organization are:

"the creation and realization of a new strategy for the development of humanity which meets global civilization challenges ('reduction of population, using the resources of the planet with enslaved human control and other agendas,' St. Germaine added);

"the creation of optimal conditions promoting the spiritual enlightenment of humanity ('meaning dark spirited agenda, falsely enlightened, thinking they are the only enlightened ones,' St. Germaine added);

"and the realization of a new futuristic reality based on 5 principles: high spirituality (St. Germaine: 'dark energy') high culture (St. Germaine: 'torture will be involved as well as sexual depravity for their enjoyment') high ethics (St. Germaine: 'their own') high science and high technologies (St. Germaine: 'true').

"The main science mega-project of the 2045 Initiative aims to create technologies enabling the transfer of a individual's personality to a more advanced non-biological carrier, and extended life, including to the point of immortality. We devote particular attention to enabling the fullest possible dialogue between the world's major spiritual traditions, science and society ('already under Cabal control,' St. Germaine added).

"A large-scale transformation of humanity, comparable to some the major spiritual and sci-tech revolutions in history, will require a new strategy. We believe this to be necessary to overcome existing crises, which threaten our planetary habitat and the continued existence of humanity as a species. With the *2045 Initiative*, we hope to realize a new strategy for humanities development, and in so doing. Create a more productive, fulfilling, and satisfying future.

"The '2045' team is working toward creating an international research center (already in place) where leading scientists will be engaged in research and development in the fields of anthropomorphic robotics, living systems modeling, and brain and consciousness modeling with the goal of transferring one's individual consciousness to an artificial carrier and achieving cybernetic immortality.

"An annual congress '*The Global Future 2045*' is organized by the *Initiative* to give platform for discussing mankind's evolutionary strategy based on technologies of cybernetic immortality as well as the possible impact of such technologies on global society, politics and economies of the future."

St. Germaine comments here. "Reading this, scientists, with their curiosity, tell themselves, 'Wow, this could be much better than what the planet is going through right now.' But what they don't realize is, they will be helping to create immortal, highly intelligence-gathering, cybernetic bodies to house the mean-spirited consciousness of the Cabal leaders of the same secret society which has caused the wars, contentions and suffering of humanity for centuries, and unleashing these creations upon an un-expecting universe to reign with 'blood and horror.'

"We will continue on from the website material," St. Germaine stated.

"Future prospects of '2045' Initiative for Society

"2015-2020

"The emergence and widespread use of affordable android 'avatars' controlled by a 'brain-computer' interface. Coupled with related technologies 'avatars' will give people a number of new features: ability to work in dangerous environments, perform rescue operations, travel in extreme situations, etc. Avatar components will be used in medicine for the rehabilitation of fully or partially disabled patients giving them prosthetic limb or recover lost senses.

"2020-2025

"Creation of an autonomous life-support system for the human brain linked to a robot, 'avatar,' will save people who's body is completely worn out or irreversibly damaged. Any patient with an intact brain will be able to return to a fully functional bodily life. Such technologies will greatly enlarge the possibility of hybrid bio-electronic devices, thus creating a new IT revolution and will make all kinds of superimposition of electronic and biological systems possible."

Message from St. Germaine:

"2025-2030

"Missing information from the web page, as the projecting remote viewers saw another world war with this technology in this space/time possibility with military 'avatars' surviving, propagating and thriving.

"2030-2035

"Creation of a computer model of the brain and human consciousness with the subsequent development of means to transfer individual consciousness onto an artificial carrier. This development will profoundly change the world, it will not only give everyone ('the governing elite,' St. Germaine added) the possibility of cybernetic immortality but will also create a friendly ('notice they are careful to add friendly,' St. Germaine added) artificial intelligence, expand human capabilities and provide opportunities for ordinary people to restore or modify their own brain multiple times. The final result at this stage can be a real revolution in the understanding of human nature that will completely change the human and technical prospects for humanity.

"2045

"This is the time when substance-independent minds will receive new bodies with capacities far exceeding those of ordinary humans. A new era for humanity will arrive! Changes will occur in all spheres of human activity – energy generation, transportation, politics, medicine, psychology, sciences, and so on.

"Today it is hard to imagine a future when bodies consisting of nano-robots will become affordable and capable of taking any form. It is also hard to imagine body holograms featuring controlled matter. One thing is clear however: humanity, for the first time in its history, will make a fully managed evolutionary transition and eventually become a new species. Moreover, prerequisites for a large scale expansion into outer space will be created as well."

St. Germaine proceeded to comment on the 2045 Initiative: "As you can see, this website is full of propaganda with the Dalai Lama holding a picture of the project with its founder Dmitry Itskov saying he supports the project. Various videos are also on the website, showing the benefits of the project, giving a false hope of ending world strife, suffering and destruction with the creation of this technology. What they don't tell you," St. Germaine added, "is that the military is also taking advantage of this technology; over a year ago, DARPA – the Pentagon's research arm – announced their own plans for creating a militarized avatar project, serving as a soldier's surrogate on the battlefield. This fighting machine will have all the capabilities of war and destruction, without the restraint of human consciousness or compassion (which is considered a weakness for military objectives).

"This whole project has the potential future possibility of destroying humans as we know them; for sure we need to evolve, but to believe we can put our life essence or consciousness, without the universal karmic law of cause and effect, into a perfected self-repairing, immortal nano-robotic creation, would have dire consequences for the entire universe. It would be similar to the Borg, of *Star Trek, The Next Generation*, who wander the universe making cyborgs out of even peaceful civilizations on every planet they encounter, saying 'Resistance is futile' and assimilating and devouring the energy and resources and continuing on their conquering of the universe without conscious compassion, love, hope, peace, or the best desires of higher states of consciousness. The whole universe is hoping to avert this potentiality.

"Just because we can create something, doesn't mean we should. Humans are the Gods, as we have within us the spark of God, that creative energy which means that whatever we set as our intent and put our attention on, we will create. Wouldn't it be better to focus that energy toward evolving into benevolent loving beings, which is the better choice, than toward becoming a nemesis of the universe?"

CHAPTER 11

Putting Our World in Divine Order

St. Germaine went on to describe the method of Divine transformation, "By design of nature, our bodies are highly adaptable. We can accelerate our adaptation using Forces of high thinking and frequencies to clear our karma, personality defects, negative thought forms and energies."

After my interaction with the Archangel Hologram cards on my trip to Mt. Shasta I did in fact order the whole set. Included as a gift with the Archangel Holograms was a decree for protection. It was so beautiful and so appropriate to St. Germaine's message to utilize forces of high thinking that I asked if I could please show it as an example in this book. The author of the decree, MaDonna Mae, provided the following introduction:

Introduction to the Sacred Flames

What is the whole purpose of Life – but to gain Mastery. We are here to become Masters of ourselves and to learn how to master and work with the Divine Currents of Energy.

We are here to learn how to create beauty, harmony and success in alignment with the Cosmic Laws, but we have been very disconnected from our Divine Roots. Working with the Sacred Flames is the way to reconnect to our Divine Roots and bring ourselves back into Divine Alignment.

What caused this problem? We started focusing outward first and rarely focus inward. But if we reverse that process and focus inward first to our I AM Presence and then outward, life changes tremendously and we begin the journey back to our "home."

The Sacred Flames are critical for bringing us back to this inward alignment with our Divine Source. We were created from the Sacred Flames. They are the incorruptible Divine Energies that are so badly needed here on earth and that we need in order to become Masters.

We have not had the wherewithal to take a spiritual shower for centuries. But when we come to the conscious use and understanding of the Sacred Fire, then we have the proper tools with which to sustain, protect, create and bring heaven to earth.

The Sacred Flames are the full-power tools that we need in order to manifest major change, for everything in creation comes from the Sacred Fire.

In repairing our DNA, in repairing the cells of all of our bodies, in clearing all that needs to be cleared, we need all of the Sacred Flames.

Repairing our DNA is one aspect of the healing that is critical, but we also need to clear and clean. There is much within our energy fields that does not belong there and that causes problems for us. These energies need to be taken out and we now are aware of the Cosmic Beings to call upon who are in charge of these energies and can clear them. Once that is done, we transmute and transform all else that needs to be done. For the Masters have said that we are responsible for every bit of energy that we have used and before we can enter into the higher dimensions, every speck of darkness has to be transmuted and transformed. This is done via the Violet Flame and the other Sacred Flames.

What a gift we have been given to be able to work with the Sacred Flames and to be able to work with them through their Sacred Flame Holograms.

What a gift we have been given to be able to use the following decree for our protection, and the protection of every constructive life form, technology, building, and all constructive things on earth.

Much more information about working with the Sacred Flames is available on –

www.livingwiththesacredflames.com

MaDonna Mae

Decree for Our Protection

Beloved Mighty I AM Presence, blaze Your Mighty Tube of Invincible Light around me, my home, my car, and every aspect of my life. Fill It with Your Invincible Purity, Your Invincible Eternal Fiery Truth of everything I want to know and the Invincible Cosmic Sacred Flame of Divine Love. Fill me with the Full Power of the Ascended Masters' Cosmic Flame of Divine Love and Illumination, down to the smallest atom of my being.

Fill me with the Invincible Cosmic Powers of the Sacred Fire from the Great Central Sun. Blaze through me Your Mighty Cosmic Violet Flame. Consume all limitations within my world and every mistake that I have ever done. Replace them with Divine Purity, Love, Light, Perfection and all of the Sacred Flames.

Consume all my discordant creations and the discordant creations of others around me. Blaze the Cosmic Violet Flame into every aspect of Nature that I have harmed in any time, space or dimension in the past, present or future. I ask for the healing of all Nature.

Mighty I AM Presence, charge my mind and bodies with Your Mighty Energy, Strength, Courage, Divine Victory and Opulence. Charge every aspect of my being and world with Your Perfection. Bring this body into Your Perfect Symmetry. Charge me with the Power of the Cosmic Divine Love so that I may safely and firmly move forward into the use of the greater Powers without interruption.

Fill me with Your Invincible Solution to every problem in my life. I ask for Sacred Fire Control of myself – and everything in my life. I command the Divine Plan fulfilled in my world. (This shows us the way out of limitation. It becomes an infallible way and means of avoiding the limitations and struggles that have bound us in the past.)

Fill me with the Ascended Master Consciousness and lead me to my ascension now. (Someday, we will stand alone with our I AM Presence and know all of its Mastery and Power. It is a point of wisdom to allow that Mastery and Power to flow through our human form to give service to Life while we are still here. It is a point of wisdom to allow that Mastery in our life so that we can create the life that we choose for our highest and best good here and now and always.)

Mighty I AM Presence, be with me as I live this day. Walk this earth with me and see that I fulfill my Divine Plan. Hold me in Your Heart and make me all that You are. (As I live within the arms of my I AM Presence, Its Power will conquer my problems.) *I AM the Heart and the Mind of the Mighty I AM.*

I call in the Sword of Blue Flame that keeps me cut free forever from all that I have ever sent out in this and all embodiments. I ask the Violet Flame to transmute all into the Light.

I call in the Triple Archangel Shield to totally surround me and every aspect of my life. I ask for the Archangels' Blessing in every aspect of my life.

I ask for the Triple Arcturian Shield to completely protect me and every aspect of my life. I ask this for all constructive people and life forms, places, buildings, technology and businesses.

I ask for the most benevolent outcome for all constructive life forms. And I ask that the Violet Flame completely saturate the Earth.

Beloved Mighty I AM Presence and K-17, keep me, my loved ones and all my activities surrounded with a wall of Blue Flame and the Cosmic Blue Lightning both within my Tube of Light and outside of it. Guard and protect me and all I call forth forever. Blaze a *"Ring Pass*

Not of Blue Flame" around me for greater protection.

I ask K-17 to send a million God Warriors, if needed, to completely surround me, my home, business, car and everything in my life so that I can not be seen, heard, felt or smelt by anything of the dark in any of its forms in any time, level, space, dimension, kingdom and realm in the past, present, future, in-between and parallel lives, except when walking and driving and then only as a human being. I ask for this Protection so that I can thrive in Divine Light and Love!

Mighty I AM Presence and Ascended Masters, seal me in Your Great Transfiguration Flame and in a Mighty Pillar of Living Violet Fire, forever sustained. Lead me to my Ascension.

Project Your Cross of White Fire before me and behind me until I am completely free.

Beloved Queen of Light, blaze the rhythmic release of your Cosmic Light Substance and clothe me in the Cosmic Light Substance of the Cosmic Christ as of a Thousand Suns.

Beloved God and Goddess of Purity, seal me in the Cosmic Purity forever. Ascended Masters, charge the Flame, Substance, Essence and Miracles from your Hearts through every cell of my mind and bodies and make me as pure as the Heart of the Great Central Sun for eternity.

Mighty Elohim, fill me with the 7 Fold Flame of Cosmic Illumination. I also call for the 7 Fold Flame of Cosmic Illumination into the brain of all humans and appropriate life forms. Seal me in the Star of Gold and Divine Victory.

Fill my Tube of Light with all of the Sacred Flames that become revolving discs of Light if needed and have Them repair and heal every aspect of myself so that I once again live in the Cosmic Divine Blueprint with which I was created.

Clothe me in a Mantle of the Sacred Flames and the Crown of the Seven Elohim. Fan the Threefold Flame within my heart so that I again stand within It.

I ask the Angels of the Sacred Flames to walk with me this day and bring as much Light and Love as possible into my life and all of Nature. Bless and heal all the Powers of Nature and the Beings of the Elements.

I ask for a thousand times more impenetrable shields of Light and Love as I go through my day.

I draw in all the Light and Light Substance from the Great Central Sun that I need and desire and more.

I ask for all the blessings that my I AM Presence wishes to give me and I ask for the blessings of the Cosmic Beings of Divine Light and Love. For all of this, I give the deepest gratitude.

Again, I would like to express my gratitude to MaDonna Mae for allowing the use of this decree and for writing an introduction to the Sacred Flames. Visit her website, www.livingwiththesacredflames.com, for more information about the Sacred Flames and the Archangel Holograms.

CHAPTER 12

Creating and Manifesting 24-Strand DNA

St. Germaine continues, "Humans, as a species, descended from the Gods, and having the spark of the creator, have been creating and manifesting since their creation. The intent to create perfected 24-strand DNA will initiate the attention to the manifestation, which will result in the creation realization. It is actually very simple.

"Because our corporal bodies are of the dust of the earth, which was created from the magma, we first call upon Mother Earth, going down deep into the magma, in our thoughts, reddish-orange in color, asking for the assistance in bringing the energy of the creative magma up through our feet to the root chakra or tailbone, coccyx Plexus up into the sacral Plexus of creation.

"We then reach high into the heavens, calling forth the golden-white light from source energy, bringing down the golden-white light through our cerebral chakra, down through the heart chakra, adding love from our heart, and down to the sacral Plexus or creative center just above the pelvic bone.

"We then call forth Archangel Zaphkiel, keeper of the Orange Flame of Creation, Ecstasy, and Compassion to bring the creative energy of the orange flame into the sacral Plexus, with the intent of creating 24 strands of perfected DNA.

"Next, we call in the Star Children, keepers of the perfected 24 strands of DNA, with the intent to place the 24 strands in every cell in our body including the blood and the lymph. As we place the 24 strands of DNA into every cell in our body, we have it open up with the intent to perfect our body, nerves, organs, hormones, glands, cells, proteins, organelles, cell membranes and mitochondria at a quantum level, manifesting the perfection of the original humans.

"We then reform the 24 strands into 12 double helixes, connecting 2 strands each, into a rotating, connected, perfected spiral, double stranded DNA, with perfected telomeres at the ends, which act as little antennae, transmitting perfection, from the quantum field and source energy, into our cells and body to reverse the aging process and evolve our bodies.

"We then proceed to braid these 12 double strand helixes into rope DNA in every cell in the body, which is strong, invincible, indestructible and impenetrable to all the toxins, petrochemicals, nano-bots and radiation which has been damaging our weakened 2 stranded DNA double helix, which it has been subjected to.

"Less than a page, and only 3 minutes a day to manifest, it is to be done 12x12 times for the effect to take place (once per day, for 144 days).

"The 24-Strand DNA manifestation will evolve humans into the enlightened beings of light, which we were intended to be!

"This is what is meant for humanity. It is your choice," St. Germaine added, "not to place unrestrained, intelligence into an immortal mechanized avatar, with desire for absolute power and domination of worlds unseen."

St. Germaine added some other discussions, which are not to be revealed at this time, leaving me to ponder all he had said.

AUTHOR'S NOTE

As I have been doing the 24-Strand DNA manifestation (I'm currently at 120), every time I complete 12 more I find my body and mind are more resilient and clear, my immune system is improving, I have less pain and am sleeping better. Formerly, pain would wake me up every night. After the 96th time, I have had no pain waking me up for the past month, which for me has been a miracle.

ABOUT THE AUTHOR

Scott R. Werner, MD, practiced medicine, starting out as an OB/GYN, but became a medical intuitive after curing his own cancer with herbs and healing energy. He gave up his medical practice to focus on the real causes of disease. He now lives in St. George, Utah, with his wife and children. Scott has used herbs, homeopathic & energetic remedies, Toning (God sounds) and natural detoxing to help improve and heal untreatable illnesses and dis-ease, helping thousands of clients. He offers intuitive medical spiritual readings for clients, putting them on the products that will help them the most. Scott currently lectures to many groups in Minnesota, Nevada, California, Iowa, Hawaii, Florida, Utah, South Dakota and Peru, teaching about herbal products, homeopathics, essential oils, energy and spiritual healing.

Connect with Scott:

Web – www.scottwerner.org or www.scottwernermd.com
Facebook.com/TakeBackYourHealth.book
Email – scott.healthlongevityinc@gmail.com
Phone for Intuitive Readings – (435) 986-0025

ALSO BY SCOTT WERNER

Take Back Your Health
(Balboa Press, 2012)

Take Back Your Health was written as a sort of oracle book and has been tested by several intuitives to vibrate in unconditional love consciousness. It is not meant to be read from cover to cover, but to be opened where you are guided each day; the modality of healing for your system and body will be revealed.

When reading chapters in *Take Back Your Health*, you will find ways to:

- Clean up and detoxify your body.
- Revitalize your organs and brain function at the cellular level.
- Intuit for yourself what you should do each day for your health.

The following excerpts give a better idea of the wisdom and healing energy the book contains:

Today I Take Back My Health.

Stop living in the illusion that others have your health as their best interest.

Live each day as if everything you do, everything you eat, everything you breathe, everything you drink, everything you say, and everything you accept as true, affects your health.

I've been practicing medicine for 28 years. My experiences have taught me that everyone needs to detox and no Medical Doctor will tell you to detox and clean up the environmental and emotional toxins in your body. They will usually prescribe another chemical to add to the toxic mess.

Physically detoxing takes commitment, but can be fun to do, too.

Set goals: With a practitioner of natural medicine, preferably one who practices kinesiology, establish a communication and a partnership. When I first started practicing chelation therapy, the dosing was always tested with kinesiology, and it always indicated that I should start slow, at a lower dose. Even well trained alternative Medical doctors follow protocols, rather than reading into the body. Luckily, I always followed my intuition, using lower doses, and moving up when the body and kidneys were ready. Every patient is different. Every patient has needs of different dosing.

Cleaning up and reinvigorating the organs of elimination is of paramount importance. The colon, digestive system, liver, lymphatics, skin, lungs and kidneys all help remove toxins from the body. Each of these organs should be supported and rebuilt while detoxing.

Inno-vita, Systemic Formulas, Standard Process, and many other professional herbal companies have professionally blended herbal products that will assist, support, and rebuild the organs of elimination. Kinesiology is the best way to test which organs need support. Blood testing only shows one moment in time, and I have found it to be highly inaccurate.

Many products on the market now are excellent oral chelators. But they still need to be tested with kinesiology.

Meta-Ex. - This product from Inno-vita is an excellent oral chelator of heavy metals. It should be dosed mainly at bedtime as chelating out heavy metals may cause fatigue.

Tox-Ex - Another Product from Inno-vita, this is an excellent combination that helps remove unnatural petrochemicals, solvents, herbicides, pesticides, insecticides, unnatural hormones and other chemicals from the body.

CLNZ - This product is from Systemic Formulas and has properties of removing petrochemicals and heavy metals from the body.

The process of skin detoxing includes foot baths with ionic electrolysis of water, mineral salt soaks, massage cleansing techniques, infrared sauna, bath soaks, skin masks and body masks. Far infrared and ultrasonic detox are also available.

Story Time:

When I was first undergoing my healing from cancer, I was told I needed to do chelation therapy. I had practiced and used this infusion therapy at Cardinal Glennon Hospital for children, in St. Louis Missouri.

We used a substance called EDTA to remove lead from children who were eating leaded paint and had lead poisoning. Most of these children also were diagnosed with a disease called Pica.

We would give them an IV with EDTA, a chemical first developed in Germany in the 1930's. This substance would chelate, or grasp onto, heavy metal molecules and bring the metals out of the body through the kidneys. It would also bring out some good molecules, which would be replaced at the end of the chelation sessions. Vitamins and minerals were added in the intravenous solution.

In Arizona at that time of my experience with the cancer, homeopathic and naturopathic physicians and osteopathic doctors were the only ones doing chelation therapy.

I sought out and started doing chelation therapy. After the first few chelations, I was left with severe fatigue due to the strain on my kidneys, but I found the more chelation I did, the more energy my body seemed to have.

Then I noticed I was remembering names of people; this had been a huge frustration for me, as I could not remember the names of new acquaintances. This renewed memory capability showed me that some marvelous things were happening within my nervous system, getting the lead and other heavy metals out. I also had "downwinder," radiation isotope poisoning from above- ground nuclear bomb testing, other heavy metals, and chemical poisons. I started studying about these in my spare time. I found I could benefit from other natural substances such as chlorophyll, cilantro, N-Acetyl Cysteine, and many others.

My sister, Sharon, developed a metastatic hepatosarcoma two years after my malignant melanoma was cured. She chose to be treated via the Medical route, with chemotherapy, surgery and radiation. Within eighteen months, she died from her treatment.

I have found detoxing, nutritional supplementation and chelation therapy with EDTA and natural substances to be very beneficial.

This can be done in conjunction with the medical treatments suggested by your doctor to improve the outcome.

Today I Build My Faith

What is Faith? Biblically speaking, it's a belief in something I can't see, feel, hear, taste or touch. But if I have Faith the size of a mustard seed, I can move mountains.

Faith is belief that is not based on proof or double-blind studies.

Faith is focused belief, knowledge, power that builds from intent, and thought.

Faith builds as I add to the strength of my belief, intent and thought.

Faith changes belief into reality.

Faith transforms and transmutes energy.

The power of Faith channels through to my soul and manifests into my emotional and mental bodies, and then into the physical self.

Faith builds with my thoughts and alignment with universal truth.

My Faith aligns me with the universe.

Faith healers and natural healers are born with or develop the power to assist me with channeling the healing energy from God or Source energy.

I am born with the ability, opportunity and task of increasing my Faith and power for helping heal myself, the tribe, the planet, the universe, all of humanity.

The Masters are called Masters because they have mastered the perfect channeling of Faith, transforming energy, thought and intent. They are in perfect alignment with the universe, omnipresent, omnipotent, with perfect knowledge.

Today, I increase my Faith, and heal, aligning myself with my highest good.

Story Time:

Three years ago, Vicki and our two youngest children vacationed on a cruise to Alaska with a group from Hay House (Louis Hay's publishing company). One of my Favorite writers is Gregg Braden, and one of Vicki's is Carolyn Myss. We wanted to meet them on the trip. We said a little prayer prior to departing with that intent, expressing Faith or believing it would happen.

Prior to departing, everyone on the ship put on life vests and gathered around their lifeboats. Vicki and the girls were put with the women, and I was with the men. Gregg Braden was on my left, and Carolyn Myss was on Vicki's right side. We were both able to talk with our favorite authors for about forty minutes, right at the beginning of the cruise on the boat. Aren't Faith and manifestation wonderful? We certainly thought so!

The whole trip was filled with amazing healing and stories of Faith. As we were cruising on the ship, we entered a fjord in Alaska where the Hubbard Glacier was located. There was a thick fog and we were unable to even see the sides of the fjord. All of the people on the cruise were very spiritually oriented. It was our desire to clear the fog so we could see the glacier. A group of about 40 of us were up on the top deck manifesting to clear the fog. The power of the combined energies of those on the deck started to push the fog back away from the front of the boat and as we moved forward the fog was pushed back clear to the sides of the bay and it cleared in front of us totally. As we approached the glacier everyone cheered; we were all very happy and enjoyed the beauty and marvelous glacier and the mountains of Alaska in front of us.

When you express your Faith, more miracles can manifest in the daily processes of your life!

Today I do Kundalini Breathing

The "root lock" is a conscious contraction of the pubo-coccygeus muscle, or PC muscle, which is a hammock-like muscle, found in both sexes, that stretches from the pubic bone to the coccyx (tail bone). It forms the floor of the pelvic cavity and supports the pelvic organs. It is part of the levator ani group of muscles. When contracted it can stop the flow of urine and cut off our stool. Strengthening this muscle improves blood flow to the sexual organs and the root organs of the anus and the coccyx bone. The other important function of this muscle is that it is very active during orgasm and sexual intercourse.

Tightening of this muscle and holding this pubo-coccygeus muscle tight is called the root lock. The sacrum and coccyx bones act as a fulcrum pump, circulating the cerebral-spinal fluid or central nervous system fluid. Each layer or each chakra going up the spine and into the head acts to circulate this cerebral-spinal fluid. Having the intent to make this fluid flow is very important with kundalini breathing.

I breathe in a deep breath and ground the root chakra into the earth preferably into the magma of the earth.

Then, I breathe out, and then take another deep breath focusing energy on connecting to the heavens.

In cranial-sacral therapy, the coccyx and the sacrum act as a fulcrum, pumping cerebral-spinal fluid of the anterior spinal column into the brain and around to the posterior part of the brain and down the posterior spinal column. Pushing or thrusting the pelvis forward activates this pumping action.

Next I take a big deep breath connected to the earth and the heavens and draw in the prana of the universe, locking the root lock as the breath comes in and pushing the pelvis and sacrum forward, holding the breath for ten seconds. As the breath is released the root lock is also released. This breath is then repeated at least two more times (it can be done as many as I desire, but at least three times total for each chakra).

When I have completed at least three breaths with my root chakra doing the root lock each time as I breathe in and holding it till I release my breath, the energy is then brought up my body into the tongue, then the tongue is placed at the roof of the mouth (mid-palate) bringing the energy up. I then roll my eyes up, lifting the energy with my hands high above my head bringing the energy with the hands and locking the energy into the ninth chakra eight to twelve inches above the head.

Next, I focus on the creative, or sexual chakra. I take a big deep breath in through the nose again connected to the earth and the heavens and draw in the prana of the universe. This breath is focused on the sexual organs and a pelvic thrust is done as the breath is drawn in and held for ten seconds holding the root lock the entire time. As the breath is released the root lock is also released and the pelvis is brought back to a resting position. This is then repeated at least twice or more additional times taking care to lock the root lock and force the pelvis forward with each breath.

When I have completed at least three breaths with my pelvic chakra, doing the root lock each time as I breathe in and holding it till I release my breath, the energy is then brought up my body into the tongue, then the tongue is placed to the roof of the mouth bringing the energy up and rolling the eyes up, taking the hands high above my head and locking the energy into the ninth chakra.

I focus next on the solar plexus or abdominal chakra. I take a big deep breath in through the nose connecting to the earth and the heavens and draw in the Love of the universe. This breath is focused on the abdominal organs of the liver, pancreas, spleen, intestines, and stomach within this chakra. As the breath is brought in, I turn the entire body, with the hands over the bellybutton, to the right and hold the root lock. The breath is held for ten seconds and then released as I turn to the left. The twisting motion is right at the level of the solar plexus or just two fingerbreadths above the bellybutton. At least two additional breaths or more can be done at this level turning each time to the right and releasing when going to the left.

When I have completed at least three breaths with my solar plexus chakra, doing the root lock each time as I breathe in and holding it till I release my breath, the energy is then brought up my body into the tongue, then the tongue is placed at the roof of the mouth (mid-palate) bringing the energy up and rolling the eyes up, taking the hands high above my head bringing the energy with the hands and locking the energy into the ninth chakra, eight to twelve inches above my head.

The next level is the heart chakra. When breathing in, the body is tilted to the right at the level of the heart and locking the root lock as the breath is coming again holding the breath for 10 seconds. For the release the body is tilted to the left and the root lock is released as the breath is released. At least two additional breaths or more can be done at this level, tilting to the right with the breath coming in and the root lock locked, holding for 10 seconds, then tilting to the left and releasing.

When I have completed at least three breaths with my heart chakra, doing the root lock each time as I breathe in and holding it till I release my breath, the energy is then brought up my body into the tongue, then the tongue is placed at the roof of the mouth (mid-palate) bringing energy up and rolling the eyes up, taking the hands high above my head bringing the energy with the hands and locking the energy into the ninth chakra, eight to twelve inches above my head.

The next level is the level of the throat chakra. With this breath, when breathing into the body from the universe and the earth, the shoulders are lifted when breathing in and the root lock tightened. This is held for 10 seconds and then released as I lower the shoulders and release the root lock. This is repeated two more times lifting the shoulders up and tightening the root lock with the breath in for 10 seconds and then releasing the root lock in the shoulders at the end of the breath.

When I have completed at least three breaths with my throat chakra, doing the root lock each time as I breathe in and holding it till I release my breath, the energy is then brought up my body into the tongue, then the tongue is placed at the roof of the mouth (mid-palate) bringing the energy up and rolling the eyes up, taking the hands high above my head bringing the energy with the hands and locking the energy into the ninth chakra, eight to twelve inches above my head.

The next level is at the level of the third eye or pituitary chakra. The head will be rotated to the right while bringing in the breath and locking the root lock, and rotated to the left while releasing the breath and the root lock. This is repeated two more times or more if desired, rotating the head to the right as the breathing comes in and locking the root lock and then releasing the root lock and the breath as the rotation goes to the left. This is done in a rotating fashion in order to rotate the cerebral-spinal fluid.

When I have completed at least three breaths with my third eye chakra, doing the root lock each time as I breathe in and holding it till I release my breath, the energy is then brought up my body into the tongue, then the tongue is placed at the roof of the mouth (mid-palate) bringing the energy up and rolling the eyes up, taking the hands high above my head bringing the energy with the hands and locking the energy into the ninth chakra, eight to twelve inches above my head.

The next level is the level of the celestial chakra or pineal gland chakra. My intent is to bring in the prana of heaven and earth with the breath as my head is tilted back and my arms are extended back as if spreading out a set of wings.

The breath is held for ten seconds with the energy entering into my pineal gland and then released as my arms are brought forward and my head is tilted forward. If my neck is stiff or if this is painful, I am gentle to my neck and myself. It is important that comfort and bliss accompany this breathing. This breath should be repeated two or more times bringing the arms and head back gently, bringing in the prana and the breath and holding the root lock locked, and releasing the root lock and releasing the breath bringing the arms forward and the head forward.

When I have completed at least three breaths with my cerebral chakra, doing the root lock each time as I breathe in and holding it till I release my breath, the energy is then brought up my body into the tongue, then the tongue is placed at the roof of the mouth (mid-palate) bringing the energy up and rolling the eyes up, taking the hands high above my head bringing the energy with the hands and locking the energy into the ninth chakra, eight to twelve inches above my head.

This is a gentle exercise. If any of the root locks or chakras cause pain, the actions should be minimized and gently done till discomfort or pain is gone.

The energy stored in my ninth chakra is there for my use to heal my body or to heal someone else should I choose. This energy is released with my intent to release the energy and brought down into any part of the body to heal. I can give myself energy, as needed, or heal an organ that is particularly causing problems. I can also throw the energy to someone else using my hands if they are in need.

Story Time:

Our daughter was living in Tooele, Utah and had decided to move back home. My wife went up to help her move, and was driving home to southern Utah when she experienced severe fatigue and felt like the flu was coming on with severe headache and body aches. She called me to talk to her as she continued driving home to keep her awake and safe. I had just talked about the kundalini breathing and had stored the energy in my ninth chakra. The thought came to me to just send her that energy, to help her stay awake and drive home safely. I took my hands and put them above my head releasing a ball of energy and I threw it to her in Beaver, Utah. She was still on the phone and I asked her how she felt. She said all of a sudden her energy had improved and she was no longer sleepy. I told her to call me again if she needed the energy. She safely drove home with plenty of energy over the next two hours. Whatever is going on in your life or the life of your loved ones, this energy is readily available for you. It also can be used for whatever your body is lacking or desires.

I also have a CD explaining and leading the kundalini breathing. This is available for those who need an audio explanation of the kundalini breathing.